Ramadan Progress Tracker and Health Journal

Healing Central

Copyright © 2022

All rights reserved.

`Without limiting rights under the copyright reserved above, no part of this publication may be reproduced, stored, introduced into a retrieval system, distributed or transmitted in any form or by any means, including without limitation photocopying, recording, or other electronic or mechanical methods, without the prior written permission of the publisher, except in the case of brief quotations embodied in critical reviews and certain other non-commercial uses permitted by copyright law.

This book, with the opinions, suggestions and references made within it, is based on the author's personal experience and is for personal study and research purposes only. This program is about health and vitality, not disease. The author makes no medical claims. If you choose to use the material in this book on yourself, the author and publisher take no responsibility for your actions and decisions or the consequences thereof..

The scanning, uploading, and/or distribution of this document via the internet or via any other means without the permission of the publisher is illegal and is punishable by law. Please purchase only authorized editions and do not participate in or encourage electronic piracy of copyrightable materials

Contents Page

The Benefits of Fasting	7
How to use This Tracker	11
Suhoor	18
Ways to Open your Fasts	21
Layla Tul Qadr	29
Qur'an Tracker	30
Ramadan Tracker	34
Monthly Recap	95
Notes	96

"Allah (Subhanahu wa Ta'ala) has made Ramadan fasting obligatory. I have made the night prayer (taraweh) sunnah. He who fasts and observes night prayers believing the virtues and seeking his reward from Allah (Subhanahu wa Ta'ala), He will be saved from his sins as a newborn baby." (Nasai)

Abu Hurayrah reported that the Messenger of Allah (peace and blessings be upon him) said:

Every action a son of Adam does shall be multiplied - a good action by ten times its value, up to 700 times. Allah says: With the exception of fasting, which belongs to Me, and I reward it accordingly. For, one abandons his desire and food for My sake.

There are two occasions of joy for a fasting person: one when he breaks his fast, and the other when he meets his Lord, and the (bad) breath (of a fasting person) is better in the sight of Allah than the fragrance of musk.
(Al-Bukhari)

Abu Hurayrah reported that the Prophet (peace and blessings be upon him) said:

Fasting is a shield; so when one of you is fasting he should neither indulge in obscene language nor should he raise his voice in anger. If someone attacks him or insults him, let him say: "I am fasting!" (Muslim)

The Benefits of Fasting

As you may be aware or have experienced first hand, there are multiple benefits to dry fasting (fasting without water). From feedback received through clients, the month of Ramadan has always arrived just at the right time, i.e. to take a "foodcation" (food vacation)! This much needed break from food is exactly what your body needs in order for it to press the reset button.

Besides the spiritual benefits of Ramadan, we are treated to the invaluable opportunity of allowing our body to eliminate toxins and any weak matter that has accumulated over time. Some of the fasting health benefits include:

1 - Improving the functionality of organs. As the body fasts, the elimination of excess mucus and weak cells that are not performing can commence.

2 - Deplaquing of capillaries and arteries (to an extent but this point is dependant on the foods consumed at Iftar and Sehri).

3 - Self cleansing of the gut walls for improved vitamin absorption (again, dependant on the foods consumed before and after the fasts).

4 - Slows down aging. The body does not feel the stress from constantly having to break down and process foods.

5 - Increases levels of a brain hormone known as brain-derived neurotrophic factor (BDNF). A deficiency has been implicated in depression/anxiety.

6- Relaxes the soul. This is because the fast deplagues your intestines allowing your body to absord minerals and vitamins into the blood stream thus gaining mental clarity.

However, for these benefits to take place and be fully experienced - the fast MUST be opened correctly at Iftar time.

After a day of fasting, the kidneys are ready to eliminate acidic waste and toxins, and so at this point, it is important that the right food and drink is consumed. More information can be found in the 'Ways to open your fast' section.

Note: We recommend that you limit/remove wheat and dairy based foods from your diet during Ramadan or any other Sunnah/Nafil fasts throughout the year. Instead, focus on whole foods such as fruit, vegetables (and fish/red meat sparingly). Dairy, wheat/flour is very harsh on the gut and it will contribute towards constipating and congesting your system instead of deplagueing old mucus as stated above. It is the sustained intake of these food types that leads to chronic disease. The right food that Allah (Subhanahu wa ta'ala) has provided for us, whole, from the land, truly is the real medicine.

When an infant becomes ill, the immediate and most

natural reaction is for them to start fasting. This survival mechanism has been hardwired into us, for the sole purpose of supporting the healing process. The scientific reason behind this reaction is down to your body's ability to manage energy levels. The process of eating and digestion consumes energy and if you are ill, it will be wise for your body to limit energy expenditure on food consumption and processing it. Instead it can utilise this vital energy for healing and recovery. This may be why you lose your appetite during a severe illness. Sadly, some adults may still choose to eat foods that are not recommended in their condition - regardless of the signs, but this tends to be due to their environment and habits.

Following this raw vegan protocol (hydrating, eating fruit, and vegetables) during an illness will help you overcome it sooner than later. Alternatively, continuing to eat the "foods you love", will simply risk prolonging the healing process and/or worsening the condition.

The diet of the Prophet (Peace Be Upon Him) was one of balance and scarcity, in which raw, whole foods were eaten and meat/fish were more of a delicacy - with the backdrop of regular fasting, and physical activity (including exercise and prayer). This was the natural eating path intended for human beings. Modern-day science is also starting to come to these conclusions (reference: Dr Mark Hyman/The Pegan Diet).

It is important that we use Ramadan to improve our dietary habits. Currently, we are seeing an increase in sickness around the world. Chronic disease (cancer, diabetes, heart disease, kidney disease, obesity) cases are soaring as we continue to blindly eat the foods that society sells to us. We are also not reproducing like our ancestors once did (2+ generations back) and this is directly related to the foods we consume as how they make us feel (no clarity, groggyness, fatique, anxiety). Ramadan is only a month in the year, so take advantage of this short lived time to start making changes.

How to Use This Tracker

Read through the tips and advice throughout the following pages in order to help you to prepare for Ramadan. Each book in the series will contain information on a variety of health topics, along with discussions on the most effective practices that can support improved health and vitality. We also address the many misconceptions relating to foods.

The prophetic practices found in Hadiths and Seerah relating to facilitating and maintaining balanced health will also be highlighted throughout this series of books.

As we know, there are many different ways one is able to earn reward during Ramadan, such as fasting, praying, reading Qur'an, carrying out good deeds, donating to charity, serving food to those that have fasted and so on. This tracker allows you to record all of your efforts.

Recording your progress and activities is powerful because it supports self improvement and personal growth, whilst subconsciously pushing you to do more. The goal here is to maximise our achievements during this blessed month, and journaling your journey is in itself a rewarding action.

The Prophet (Peace Be Upon Him) said, "The most beloved of deeds to Allah are those that are most consistent, even if it is small"

- Bukhaari and Muslim

The aim is to make your Ramadan more productive and visible so you can observe and track your progress - and Insha'Allah see improvements as the days go on. It is also to create new and improved habits, all while you are tracking your ongoing progress. As your routine adapts with new positive actions, these habits will Insha'Allah become habitual and become part of your daily lives beyond the month of Ramadan.

We recommend that you complete your journal along with friends and family members as this will contribute towards better and more meaningful results. You can also push each other to doing more and create new ideas of good deeds to perform. For example, you may cook an Iftar meal for the local masjid, and another friend/family member may decide to cook a dish for the neighbours. The results and goodness can be amplified through a group effort, whilst one motivates the other.

We have included a section on how to open your fasts and the foods that are healthier to consume as well as foods that may not serve you as well. It is very tempting and easy to think that after a full day of fasting that your body requires excessive food, but this merely leads to unhealthy eating and glutony. We must exercise some control after a day of fasting in order to maximise the benefits of the fast.

Having experimented with a variety of different diets on clients (ketogenic, vegan, paleolithic, pescitarian, frutarian, carnivore), we have come to the conclusion that the most balanced and healthy dietary protocol is that of our beloved prophet Muhammad (Peace Be Upon Him).

By following the Sunnah way of eating, you will feel increased mental clarity and physical health benefits. Dependant on the condition, it may subside. We have noticed that as the health and wellbeing of a patient/client improves, any conditions that they may have been struggling with previously, started to resolve.

Within our Ramadan tracker and journals, we have laid out each page in a way that will allow you to record and track your progress. It has been made easy for you to review and refer to your previous records and subsequent progress.

To serve as a reminder, we have included a checklist of all the Fard (compulsory) prayers and Sunnah (recommended) prayers. Insh'Allah this will support and increase you in your Deen.

"Allah will build a house in Paradise for a person who performs twelve rak'ah of prayers other than fard prayers during the day and night. They are the following prayers: two rak'ahs before the morning prayer, four rak'ahs before the noon prayer, two rak'ahs after the noon prayer, two rak'ahs after the evening prayer and two rak'ahs after the night prayer."

- Tirmidhi; Salat, 189; Nasai, Qiyamul-Layl, 66; Ibn Majah, Iqama, 100

Use the Qur'an tracker to record how much you have read

each day. Make an effort to try and increase the amount read everyday, even it is just one more verse, and keep it consistent.

Completing the Qur'an in Ramadan is not obligatory for the fasting person, but one should read it as much as possible as there is not only a great deal of reward to be gained from it but it was the Sunnah of our Prophet (Peace Be Upon Him). It is also a good opportunity to track what one is capable of achieving, especially if you are striving to complete it before Ramadan ends. It was the practice of the companions (may Allah be pleased with them) to strive to complete the Qur'an in Ramadan, following the example of the Prophet (Peace Be Upon Him).

Al-Bukhaari (4614) from Abu Hurayrah (may Allah be pleased with him) who said: Jibreel used to review the Qur'an with the Prophet (Peace Be Upon Him) once every year, and he reviewed it with him twice in the year in which he passed away.

We have included a Quranic verse for each day, with transliteration and translation as a guide for easier reading and understanding. If one is busy with other duties then it is encouraged to find time to read just that one verse. For beginners, it is recommended to read the Qur'an's Arabic whilst being supervised by either a teacher or somebody who reads the Qur'an with correct Tajweed. The transliterion is intended as more of a guide for overall letter and word recognition for those new to Arabic. Regular practice will improve your confidence, and Insha'Allah very soon, it will become easier for you to read through each daily verse.

You can write down what you want to achieve for that day and then record whether it was achieved of not. You may want to learn a new Du'a or memorize a verse of the Qur'an, listen to a lecture and so on. If that task was not completed, then ask yourself why it was not? What was it that prevented you from completing that task? Were you busy doing something that pleased Allah (Subhanahu wa ta'ala)? Were you doing something else that could help you grow as a person? If you die tomorrow, would you be pleased with how you spent your last day? These questions are there help you become more mindful and conscious as a person, and to be aware of how productively you are spending your day.

When fasting, you will come to find that you have a lot more time on your hands, so the question is, how are you spending that new found time, and is this time being filled with activities that please Allah (Subhanahu wa ta'ala)?

A Daily Checklist is provided to keep track of good deeds performed. It is not neccesry to complete of all of them, but seen more as a productivity list of what one is capable of achieving and if you find nothing is ticked, then allow yourself to focus on just one task to achieve for that day. A small charitable donation earns more reward than doing nothing. Discover new ones and record them in the notes section.

Notes section: This area is simply for you to add anything extra you wish to keep track of. You may want to learn something new and track your progress. You can also use this as a food and thoughts diary and monitor how you feel after each day. You could even note down what you ate for dinner and how you felt. Be moderate in eating where possible.

Was a heavy meal a hindrance on your night prayers? Did you feel hungrier the following day as a result of eating too much? How did you feel eating a moderate portion in comparison? Did you have more energy the following day? Are you losing excess body fat, and is this progress helping you reflect on how to best improve your regular diet? Are your hunger pangs more controllable as a result of fasting and eating raw/whole foods? The following pages will detail how to open your fasts according to the Sunnah and Insha'Allah help you see and feel positive results.

Keep your house clean, for a tidy house makes way for a clear mind. You can declutter anything you havent used in a long time. If you were stranded on a desert island, would you really need everything you own? If your possessions dissapeared tomorrow, how many items would you be able to remember off the top of your head? Simplify your life, for when we leave it, it will be best to leave behind knowledge, good deeds, and pious children, as opposed to material items that would be left for other people to sort.

Ibn 'Umar (may Allah be pleased with him) narrated that the Messenger of Allah (peace and blessings be upon him) said: " May Allah have mercy on the person whom prays four (Rak'ahs) before Asr. "

Suhoor

Suhoor is the time before sunrise. During this short space of time, one is able to drink and eat, right before the fast commences. There may be Muslims that skip this sacred time of the day, but the Prophet (Peace Be Upon Him) told us of the goodness and bounties found within Suhoor:

"Have Suhoor even if it is a mouthful of water."
(Ibn Hibban)

"Indeed Allah and His angels send Salah upon those who have Suhoor." (Tabarani)

"Indeed it is a blessing that Allah (Subhanahu wa ta'ala) has given to all of you, so do not leave it." (Nasai)

Foods consumed during Suhoor needs to be thought out because it is very easy to consume foods one would normally eat or drink on an ordinary day. Alternatively, one might take this as an opportunity to eat whatever they desire and the last opportunity to consume it before a long day of fasting begins. However, eating this way is actually detrimental to your body, and dependent on the volume of food you consume, you will suffer from severe hunger pangs later on in the morning.

Do note that Suhoor is not a time for you to have a breakfast buffet (e.g. bowls of processed sugar-packed cereals). Processed foods and foods packed with sugars will aggressively spike insulin in your body and as it fights to bring sugar levels back in line, you will feel undesirable cramps and hunger sensations. Sugars found in whole foods will release far more slowly and this will leave you in a better position overall. Eating foods such as porridge with milk, and granola cereal/bars is another "healthy eating" misconception in today's society.

Oats cooked in today's cows milk will contain the inflammatory protein Casein A1, and this is damaging to vitality and good health. You could instead try goat's milk which does not contain this protein. Granola on the other hand is packed with refined sugar which again spike insulin. Another favourite is peanut butter on toast - peanut butter contains lectins and these have been found to cause cancerous cells within mice. Today's bread is another concern. Over time, and with GMO and chemical processes becoming involved in the food manufacturing industry, the wheat that we have today has become harsh on our digestive tract - not to mention the existence of Gluten, another protein, which is damaging to the gut lining.

We have been asked about milk and some have said that milk and wheat were a staple of the prophetic diet. Whilst this is true, the quality of both wheat and dairy was of a much higher standard. Present day, we see a multitude of hormones, antibiotics and various chemicals being filtered through to our dairy products. Wheat has been genetically modified and it does not digest as well as it once did - contributing towards one of the root causes behind chronic disease (a leaky/damaged gut).

Nutritionists are discovering that allergies and illnesses have a correlation with wheat and dairy products. We are keen on reinforcing this message - try to work towards eliminating wheat, and dairy based food products.

During Ramadan, if possible, do your best to keep your food intake moderate to low, with a special focus on fruits and vegetables. You could eat some dates and other fruits that are available. Some clients enjoy a plate of carrots and cucumbers as a breakfast meal as they are nutritious, filling and allows for easy bowel movements to take place. You could also make smoothies and juices using fruits and vegetables. Experiment and have fun with it.

Ways to open your fast:

Dua to open fast:

اللّهُمَّ إِنِّى لَكَ صُمْتُ وَبِكَ آمَنْتُ [وَعَلَيْكَ تَوَكَّلْتُ] وَعَلَى رِزْقِكَ أَفْطَرْتُ

Allahumma inni laka sumtu wa bika aamantu wa alayka tawakkaltu wa ala rizq-ika-aftartu

O Allah! I fasted for You and I believe in You and I put my trust in You and I break my fast with Your sustenance

It was narrated from Abu Hurayrah that the Messenger of Allah (Peace Be Upon Him) said: "The people will remain upon goodness so long as they hasten to break the fast. Hasten to break the fast, for the Jews delay it."

"The Messenger of Allah (Peace Be Upon Him) would break the fast with fresh dates before performing Salah. If there were no fresh dates then (he would break the fast) with dried dates, and if there were no dried dates then he would take a few sips of water." (Tirmidhi)

After a long dry fast, your body (and kidneys) needs to be awakened in a gentle manner. Stuffing yourself during Iftar with food and drink, until you feel sick, in order to make up for a day of fasting is sadly an all too common occurrence. That is like shocking somebody into waking up in the morning! This puts an incredible strain on your organs but most importantly on your kidneys. After a long fast, the kidneys are primed to eliminate your body's toxins and so this is not a time to be throwing in a ton of dehydrating food - instead, hydration (with electrolytes) is required. Not to mention that by expanding your stomach with each Iftar, you will expose yourself to the trap of desiring more, and more food.

Initially, during the first week of fasting, your stomach will be contracting and reducing down in size, as it adapts to the new dietary regimen. During this time, the hunger pangs that you experience may feel aggressive and unbearable but these feelings can be managed. The aim is to gently feed the body small amounts of foods that are whole and were intended for our species. Eating uncontrollably will only lead to a re-expansion of the stomach and re-enter you into the cycle of feeling hunger pangs.

We recognise that it can be difficult to detach from foods rich in wheat, including breads, cereals, waffles, cakes, biscuits. However, it should be noted that historically, starches from wheat were used as a glue to bind the spines of books. Furthermore, if you mix some flour in water - whether that be for the purposes of making "play-doh" or chapattis - you will notice that the wet dough is like a glue that just won't leave your hands easily, even after scrubbing them under water. Just imagine how your body copes with such foods. The point is that it does not cope well at all and the gut ends up suffering through developing plaque and damage.

In order to undo previous damage and congestion within the gut, we simply need to turn back to what was intended for us within our beautiful Deen. Modern day science is now starting to find incredible benefits in specific foods that were already mentioned within our scriptures. Pomegranates, olives, amongst others, including green tea, contain compounds called phenols, which are antioxidants that have an array of anti-inflammatory properties. These foods are true healers and so it is even more miraculous that they had such a focus placed on them over 1400 years ago.

We have been asked about milk and some have said that milk and wheat were a staple of the prophetic diet. Whilst this is true, the quality of both wheat and dairy was of a much higher standard. Present day, we see a multitude of hormones, antibiotics and various chemicals being filtered through to our dairy products. Wheat has been genetically modified and it does not digest as well as it once did - contributing towards one of the root causes behind chronic disease (a leaky/damaged gut).

Another cause for concern is the mixing of foods containing sugars (carbohydrates) and fats. For example, a burger will have the carbohydrates/sugars coming in from the bread bun and the fat from the fillet. Unfortunately, the body struggles with processing such food combinations and this simply results in fat being stored around the waist (protection mechanism to guard the vital organs), and amongst internal organs and arteries. Making your body work harder during digestion causes oxidative stress, which subsequently leads to accelerated aging.

Here are some examples of reliable water-dense fruits that can support your inner cleanse during Iftar: mangos, pomegranates, red seeded grapes, plums, watermelons, citrus fruits (e.g. oranges, tangerines, grapefruits). Malabsorption is a major problem within society today. We are just not absorbing the nutrients from the foods that we eat because our guts are compromised and congested.

Water-dense fruits are powerful in terms of fermenting plaque off the gut walls, and this will eventually lead to an improved absorption and utilisation of nutrients from consumed foods. As you go through this self-cleansing detoxification (and regeneration) process, your health and vitality should grow to a point where it is able to out-muscle and overpower any previous conditions/diseases that were lurking. Hormone levels and deficiencies should rebalance and your blood should also become cleaner, insha'Allah.

It is also worth mentioning that as human beings, we do not actually require a huge amount of food in order to maintain good health. For example, a baby grows and flourishes just off small doses of mother's milk. Allah (Subhanahu wa ta'ala) made us robust hence why it was recently found that the human race evolved through food scarcity. This is further highlighted in the following quote:

Miqdam ibn Ma'd reported: The Messenger of Allah, peace and blessings be upon him, said, "The son of Adam cannot fill a vessel worse than his stomach, as it is enough for him to take a few bites to straighten his back. If he cannot do it, then he may fill it with a third of his food, a third of his drink, and a third of his breath."

Our body has been entrusted upon us by Allah SWT and therefore we must make every effort to take care of it, so that we can continue to serve Allah (Subhanahu wa ta'ala) in good health. Insh'Allah.

The following are example daily plans that we prescribed to clients during Ramadan (or any other fast throughout the year):

Typical day plan:

1) The priority should be correctly hydrating yourself. Between 1 and 3 litres (depending on your weight/body composition) of spring water along with a few dates is a good start.

2) Water-dense laxative fruits (e.g. pineapples, mangos, grapes, apples, pears, pomegranates, melons, figs, oranges, plums, dates, prunes) should follow shortly after. This process will help flush out the fast's accumulated toxins. Note: after a long dry fast, a "laxative fruit" is necessary because fasts can cause constipation. This needs to be coupled with water, to help flush it through the system.

3) Staying busy with prayer and movement is a key to maintaining this way of eating. Once you get into a routine,

you will find that it's actually quite easy to complete Ramadan this way. Give it a try and see the results for yourself. Insha'Allah you will be impressed.

4) Eat the fruit and vegetables until your heart's content. We have found with patients that when bananas (burrow range preferred because they are less inclined to be genetically modified), mangoes and dates were consumed, they would be satisfied for a longer period of time. This is also related to the fact that these fruits are higher in calories.

5) We do not want to expand the stomach with cooked foods. This will not only make it harder to pray that night but the following day's fast will also be filled with avoidable hunger pangs.

6) It is kinder to the fasting person to eat raw and uncooked foods (predominantly fruits and vegetables) as this will offer you improved strength for worship. Eating a healthy, light meal for Iftar will give you the ability to perform Taraweeh (night prayers) without feeling too full or tired from overeating, insha'Allah.

7) Drinking a sufficient volume of water is very important. We prefer good quality spring water because its more natural and kinder to the kidneys.

8) Insh'Allah you will start to see health improvements within days. Our patients noted that they felt more supple and had superior mental clarity as a result of eating high

energy, live/uncooked foods.

For the average healthy person, we recommend that you do your best to stick to the above meal plan in order to give your body the break it needs from any previous unhealthy foods. This is a good opportunity to detoxify, cleanse and heal your body. However, if you feel that you are not capable of this protocol, and you are not yet convinced of the health benefits that will follow, then we have an alternative day plan that you could follow:

Alternative day plan:

a) Open your fast with a handful of dates and warm water (you can add a few drops of honey for sweetness).

b) Take a break and go to pray Maghrib.

c) Dinner time! Choose from either fish or red meat (beef preferred as the majority of cows graze off grass and so we stand to gain from this beneficial nutrition) or eggs - accompanied with a large salad bowl, consisting of leafy greens (kale, spinach, greens) and vegetables (carrots, cabbage, cucumber, lettuce, broccoli) sprinkled with pink salt (for mineral and electrolyte value) and freshly squeezed lemon juice. Start by including the vegetables that you enjoy most and add more as you go on.

d) If this is initially not satisfying you sufficiently, you could increase the amount you eat but also add olive oil. This is a healthy oil to consume (uncooked).

e) In the early stages, we allow for snacks. These can include specific nuts and dried fruit. Pecan nuts, walnuts, hazel nuts, macadamia nuts, almonds - are reasonable options. We wouldn't recommend peanuts or cashew nuts as these contain lectins. We have included information about lectins in the previous section.

f) Remember to keep up your water intake - a good quality spring water is preferred.

NOTE: Family gatherings can feel like a tempting time to indulge in anything and everything. Although this may not be a problem as a one off event (get back on track the following day), do your best to be controlled in the amount that you consume. Always remind yourself of the sickening and heavy feeling that you will feel afterwards and the days of hunger pangs and unnecessary desires that will follow. One idea of a healthy social snack serving would be to serve dates, dried fruits along with a herbal tea (chamomile tea, green tea, or peppermint tea).

As you start to experience the benefits of this new dietary routine, we encourage you to spread this knowledge amongst your friends and family, so they can also benefit. This is also a form of Dawah. May Allah (Subhanahu wa ta'ala) be pleased with your efforts. Ameen.

If you would like further support, guidance and coaching, please do feel free to contact us on:
healingcentral8@gmail.com

Layla Tul Qadr

Abu Hurayrah reported that the Prophet (Peace Be Upon Him) said: Whoever stands (in the voluntary night prayer) in Laylat Al-Qadr out of faith and in hope of reward, his previous sins will be forgiven. (Al-Bukhari)

Aisha (ra) said that the Prophet (Peace Be Upon Him) said "Look for Laylat al-Qadr on an odd-numbered night during the last ten nights of Ramadhan". (Bukhari).14.

`A'ishah (May Allah be pleased with her) reported: The Messenger of Allah (Peace Be Upon Him) used to strive more in worship during Ramadan than he strove in any other time of the year; and he would devote himself more (in the worship of Allah) in the last ten nights of Ramadan than he did in earlier part of the month. (Muslim).

Good deeds performed on that single night are equal to those performed over a thousand months: "The Night of Al-Qadr is better than a thousand months" (Quran 97:3).

Anas ibn Malik related that Rasulullah said: When Lailat al-Qadr comes Gabriel descends with a company of angels who ask for blessings on everyone who is remembering Allah, whether they are sitting or standing (Baihaqi).

Qur'an Tracker

Surah   **Date Completed**

1. Al-Fatihah (the Opening)   _____
2. Al-Baqarah (the Cow)   _____
3. Aali Imran (the Family of Imran)_____
4. An-Nisa' (the Women)   _____
5. Al-Ma'idah (the Table)   _____
6. Al-An'am (the Cattle)   _____
7. Al-A'raf (the Heights)   _____
8. Al-Anfal (the Spoils of War)   _____
9. At-Taubah (the Repentance)   _____
10. Yunus (Yunus)   _____
11. Hud (Hud)   _____
12. Yusuf (Yusuf)   _____
13. Ar-Ra'd (the Thunder)   _____
14. Ibrahim (Ibrahim)   _____
15. Al-Hijr (the Rocky Tract)   _____
16. An-Nahl (the Bees)   _____
17. Al-Isra' (the Night Journey)   _____
18. Al-Kahf (the Cave)   _____
19. Maryam (Maryam)   _____
20. Ta-Ha (Ta-Ha)   _____
21. Al-Anbiya' (the Prophets)   _____
22. Al-Haj (the Pilgrimage)   _____
23. Al-Mu'minun (the Believers)   _____
24. An-Nur (the Light)   _____
25. Al-Furqan (the Criterion)   _____
26. Ash-Shu'ara' (the Poets)   _____
27. An-Naml (the Ants)   _____
28. Al-Qasas (the Stories)   _____
29. Al-Ankabut (the Spider)   _____
30. Ar-Rum (the Romans)   _____
31. Luqman (Luqman)   _____
32. As-Sajdah (the Prostration)   _____
33. Al-Ahzab (the Combined Forces)_____

34. Saba' (the Sabeans) _____
35. Al-Fatir (the Originator) _____
36. Ya-Sin (Ya-Sin) _____
37. As-Saffah (Those Ranges in Ranks) _____
38. Sad (Sad) _____
39. Az-Zumar (the Groups) _____
40. Ghafar (the Forgiver) _____
41. Fussilat (Distinguished) _____
42. Ash-Shura (the Consultation) _____
43. Az-Zukhruf (the Gold) _____
44. Ad-Dukhan (the Smoke) _____
45. Al-Jathiyah (the Kneeling) _____
46. Al-Ahqaf (the Valley) _____
47. Muhammad (Muhammad) _____
48. Al-Fat'h (the Victory) _____
49. Al-Hujurat (the Dwellings) _____
50. Qaf (Qaf) _____
51. Adz-Dzariyah (the Scatterers) _____
52. At-Tur (the Mount) _____
53. An-Najm (the Star) _____
54. Al-Qamar (the Moon) _____
55. Ar-Rahman (the Most Gracious) _____
56. Al-Waqi'ah (the Event) _____
57. Al-Hadid (the Iron) _____
58. Al-Mujadilah (the Reasoning) _____
59. Al-Hashr (the Gathering) _____
60. Al-Mumtahanah (the Tested) _____
61. As-Saf (the Row) _____
62. Al-Jum'ah (Friday) _____
63. Al-Munafiqun (the Hypocrites) _____
64. At-Taghabun (the Loss & Gain) _____
65. At-Talaq (the Divorce) _____
66. At-Tahrim (the Prohibition) _____
67. Al-Mulk – (the Kingdom) _____
68. Al-Qalam (the Pen) _____
69. Al-Haqqah (the Inevitable) _____
70. Al-Ma'arij (the Elevated Passages) _____

71. Nuh (Nuh) _____
72. Al-Jinn (the Jinn) _____
73. Al-Muzammil (the Wrapped) _____
74. Al-Mudaththir (the Cloaked) _____
75. Al-Qiyamah (the Resurrection) _____
76. Al-Insan (the Human) _____
77. Al-Mursalat (Those Sent Forth) _____
78. An-Naba' (the Great News) _____
79. An-Nazi'at (Those Who Pull Out) _____
80. 'Abasa (He Frowned) _____
81. At-Takwir (the Overthrowing) _____
82. Al-Infitar (the Cleaving) _____
83. Al-Mutaffifin (Those Who Deal in Fraud) _____
84. Al-Inshiqaq (the Splitting Asunder) _____
85. Al-Buruj (the Stars) _____
86. At-Tariq (the Nightcomer) _____
87. Al-A'la (the Most High) _____
88. Al-Ghashiyah (the Overwhelming) _____
89. Al-Fajr (the Dawn) _____
90. Al-Balad (the City) _____
91. Ash-Shams (the Sun) _____
92. Al-Layl (the Night) _____
93. Adh-Dhuha (the Forenoon) _____
94. Al-Inshirah (the Opening Forth) _____
95. At-Tin (the Fig) _____
96. Al-'Alaq (the Clot) _____
97. Al-Qadar (the Night of Decree) _____
98. Al-Bayinah (the Proof) _____
99. Az-Zalzalah (the Earthquake) _____
100. Al-'Adiyah (the Runners) _____
101. Al-Qari'ah (the Striking Hour) _____
102. At-Takathur (the Piling Up) _____
103. Al-'Asr (the Time) _____
104. Al-Humazah (the Slanderer) _____
105. Al-Fil (the Elephant) _____
106. Quraish (Quraish) _____
107. Al-Ma'un (the Assistance) _____

108. Al-Kauthar (the River of Abundance) _____
109. Al-Kafirun (the Disbelievers) _____
110. An-Nasr (the Help)   _____
111. Al-Masad (the Palm Fiber)   _____
112. Al-Ikhlas (the Sincerity)   _____
113. Al-Falaq (the Daybreak)   _____
114. An-Nas (Mankind)   _____

Ramadan Day 1

Todays Goal: **Was it achieved?**

_____   _____

Quran'ic Verse of the Day

وَلَقَدْ صَدَّقَ عَلَيْهِمْ إِبْلِيسُ ظَنَّهُ فَاتَّبَعُوهُ إِلَّا فَرِيقًا مِّنَ ٱلْمُؤْمِنِينَ

Wa laqad saddaq 'alaihim Ibleesu zannnabhoo fattaba'oohu illaa fareeqam minal mu'mineen

20. And Iblees had already confirmed through them his assumption, so they followed him, except for a party of believers.

Qur'an Tracker   ## Daily Checklist

Please keep this book high up as a means of respect for it contains Islamic references.

Juz:

Surah:

Pages ___ **to** ___

○ Fast Completed

○ Prayed in Mosque: How Many Times

○ Charitable Donation

○ Spoke Kind Words all Day

○ Ate a Healthy Meal

○ Performed Taraweeh

Learnt Something New?

_____

_____

_____

Cross off prayers upon completion

Fajr
2 Sunnah
2 Fard

Zuhr
4 Sunnah
4 Fard
2 Sunnah

Asr
4 Fard

Maghrib
3 Sunnah
2 Fard

'Isha
4 Sunnah
2 Sunnah

Taraweeh
Rakats:

Tahajjud
Rakats:

Hadith of the Day
Allah's Messenger (Peace Be Upon Him) said, "The taking of a bath on Friday is compulsory for every male (Muslim) who has attained the age of puberty." Sahih al-Bukhari 879

Names of Allah

Ar-Rahmaan
The Beneficent

Meal Plan
Suhoor _____

Iftar: _____

Notes

Ramadan Day 2

Todays Goal: **Was it achieved?**

_____   _____

Quran'ic Verse of the Day

قُل لَّا تُسْـَٔلُونَ عَمَّآ أَجْرَمْنَا وَلَا نُسْـَٔلُ عَمَّا تَعْمَلُونَ

Qul laa tus'aloona 'ammaaa ajramnaa wa laa nus'alu 'ammaa ta'maloon

25. Say, "You will not be asked about what we committed, and we will not be asked about what you do."

Qur'an Tracker

Juz:
Surah:
Pages ___ **to** ___

Daily Checklist

○ Fast Completed

○ Prayed in Mosque: How Many Times

○ Charitable Donation

○ Spoke Kind Words all Day

○ Ate a Healthy Meal

○ Performed Taraweeh

Learnt Something New?

_____
_____
_____

Cross off prayers upon completion

Fajr
2 Sunnah
2 Fard

Zuhr
4 Sunnah
4 Fard
2 Sunnah

Asr
4 Fard

Maghrib
3 Sunnah
2 Fard

'Isha
4 Sunnah
2 Sunnah

Taraweeh
Rakats:

Tahajjud
Rakats:

Hadith of the Day

Ibn Umar reported: The Prophet (Peace Be Upon Him) said, "May Allah have mercy on a person who prays four cycles before afternoon prayer." Source: Sunan al-Tirmidhī 430

Names of Allah

Ar-Raheem
The Merciful

Meal Plan

Suhoor _____

Iftar: _____

Notes

Ramadan Day 3

Todays Goal: **Was it achieved?**

_____   _____

Quran'ic Verse of the Day

قُلْ يَجْمَعُ بَيْنَنَا رَبُّنَا ثُمَّ يَفْتَحُ بَيْنَنَا بِالْحَقِّ وَهُوَ الْفَتَّاحُ الْعَلِيمُ

Qul yajma'u bainanaa Rabbunaa summa yaftahu bainanaa bilhaqq; wa Huwal Fattaahul 'Aleem

26. Say, "Our Lord will bring us together; then He will judge between us in truth. And He is the Knowing Judge."

Qur'an Tracker

Juz:
Surah:
Pages ____ to ____

Daily Checklist

○ Fast Completed

○ Prayed in Mosque: How Many Times

○ Charitable Donation

○ Spoke Kind Words all Day

○ Ate a Healthy Meal

○ Performed Taraweeh

Learnt Something New?

_____
_____
_____

Cross off prayers upon completion

Fajr
2 Sunnah
2 Fard

Zuhr
4 Sunnah
4 Fard
2 Sunnah

Asr
4 Fard

Maghrib
3 Sunnah
2 Fard

'Isha
4 Sunnah
2 Sunnah

Taraweeh
Rakats:

Tahajjud
Rakats:

Hadith of the Day

Allah's Messenger (ﷺ) said, "If I had not found it hard for my followers or the people, I would have ordered them to clean their teeth with Siwak for every prayer." Sahih al-Bukhari 887

Names of Allah

Al-Malik
The Eternal Lord

Meal Plan

Suhoor

Iftar:

Notes

Ramadan Day 4

Todays Goal: **Was it achieved?**

_____   _____

Quran'ic Verse of the Day

قُلْ أَرُونِىَ ٱلَّذِينَ أَلْحَقْتُم بِهِۦ شُرَكَآءَ ۖ كَلَّا ۚ بَلْ هُوَ ٱللَّهُ ٱلْعَزِيزُ ٱلْحَكِيمُ

Qul arooniyal lazeena alhaqtum bihee shurakaaa'a kallaa; bal Huwal Laahul 'Azeezul Hakeem

27. Say, "Show me those whom you have attached to Him as partners. No! Rather, He [alone] is Allah, the Exalted in Might, the Wise."

Qur'an Tracker

Juz:
Surah:
Pages ____ to ____

Daily Checklist

◯ Fast Completed

◯ Prayed in Mosque: How Many Times

◯ Charitable Donation

◯ Spoke Kind Words all Day

◯ Ate a Healthy Meal

◯ Performed Taraweeh

Learnt Something New?

_____
_____
_____

Cross off prayers upon completion

Fajr
2 Sunnah
2 Fard

Zuhr
4 Sunnah
4 Fard
2 Sunnah

Asr
4 Fard

Maghrib
3 Sunnah
2 Fard

'Isha
4 Sunnah
2 Sunnah

Taraweeh
Rakats:

Tahajjud
Rakats:

Hadith of the Day
Narrated by Al-Bara. The bowing, the prostrations, the period of standing after bowing and the interval between the two prostrations of the Prophet used to be equal in duration. Hadith No: 766

Names of Allah

Al-Quddus
The Most Sacred

Meal Plan
Suhoor

Iftar:

Notes

Ramadan Day 5

Todays Goal: **Was it achieved?**

_____   _____

Quran'ic Verse of the Day

وَمَا أَرْسَلْنَاكَ إِلَّا كَافَّةً لِّلنَّاسِ بَشِيرًا وَنَذِيرًا وَلَٰكِنَّ أَكْثَرَ ٱلنَّاسِ لَا يَعْلَمُونَ

Wa maaa arsalnaaka illaa kaaffatal linnaasi basheeranw wa nazeeranw wa laakinna aksaran naasi laa ya'lamoon

28. And We have not sent you except comprehensively to mankind as a bringer of good tidings and a warner. But most of the people do not know.

Qur'an Tracker

Juz:
Surah:
Pages ____ **to** ____

Daily Checklist

○ Fast Completed

○ Prayed in Mosque: How Many Times

○ Charitable Donation

○ Spoke Kind Words all Day

○ Ate a Healthy Meal

○ Performed Taraweeh

Learnt Something New?

_____
_____
_____
_____

Cross off prayers upon completion

Fajr
2 Sunnah
2 Fard

Zuhr
4 Sunnah
4 Fard
2 Sunnah

Asr
4 Fard

Maghrib
3 Sunnah
2 Fard

'Isha
4 Sunnah
2 Sunnah

Taraweeh
Rakats:

Tahajjud
Rakats:

Hadith of the Day
Narrated by Abdullah bin Malik bin Buhaina. Whenever the Prophet (Peace Be Upon Him) used to offer prayer he used to keep arms away (from the body) so that the whiteness of his armpits was visible. Hadith No: 771

Names of Allah

As-Salam
The Embodiment of Peace

Meal Plan
Suhoor _____

Iftar: _____

Notes

Ramadan Day 6

Todays Goal: **Was it achieved?**

_____   _____

Quran'ic Verse of the Day

Wa yaqooloona mataa haazal wa'du in kuntum saadiqeen
29. And they say, "When is this promise, if you should be truthful?"

قُل لَّكُم مِّيعَادُ يَوْمٍ لَّا تَسْتَـْٔخِرُونَ عَنْهُ سَاعَةً وَلَا تَسْتَقْدِمُونَ

Qur'an Tracker

Juz:
Surah:
Pages ____ to ____

Learnt Something New?

_____

_____

_____

Daily Checklist

◯ Fast Completed

◯ Prayed in Mosque: How Many Times

◯ Charitable Donation

◯ Spoke Kind Words all Day

◯ Ate a Healthy Meal

◯ Performed Taraweeh

Cross off prayers upon completion

Fajr
2 Sunnah
2 Fard

Zuhr
4 Sunnah
4 Fard
2 Sunnah

Asr
4 Fard

Maghrib
3 Sunnah
2 Fard

'Isha
4 Sunnah
2 Sunnah

Taraweeh
Rakats:

Tahajjud
Rakats:

Hadith of the Day

Narrated Anas bin Malik: The Prophet (ﷺ) said, "Ad-Dajjal will come to Medina and find the angels guarding it. So Allah willing, neither Ad-Dajjal, nor plague will be able to come near it." Sahih al-Bukhari 7134

Names of Allah

Al-Mu'min
The Infuser of Faith

Meal Plan

Suhoor _____

Iftar: _____

Notes

Ramadan Day 7

Todays Goal: **Was it achieved?**

_____   _____

Quran'ic Verse of the Day

قُلْ إِنَّ رَبِّى يَبْسُطُ ٱلرِّزْقَ لِمَن يَشَآءُ وَيَقْدِرُ وَلَٰكِنَّ أَكْثَرَ ٱلنَّاسِ لَا يَعْلَمُونَ

Qul inna Rabbee yabsutur rizqa limai yashaaa'u wa yaqdiru wa laakinna aksaran naasi laa ya'lamoon (section 4)

36. Say, "Indeed, my Lord extends provision for whom He wills and restricts [it], but most of the people do not know."

Qur'an Tracker

Juz:
Surah:
Pages ___ to ___

Daily Checklist

○ Fast Completed

○ Prayed in Mosque: How Many Times

○ Charitable Donation

○ Spoke Kind Words all Day

○ Ate a Healthy Meal

○ Performed Taraweeh

Learnt Something New?

_____

_____

_____

Cross off prayers upon completion

Fajr
2 Sunnah
2 Fard

Zuhr
4 Sunnah
4 Fard
2 Sunnah

Asr
4 Fard

Maghrib
3 Sunnah
2 Fard

'Isha
4 Sunnah
2 Sunnah

Taraweeh
Rakats:

Tahajjud
Rakats:

Hadith of the Day

Abu Darda' reported Allah's Apostle (ﷺ) as saying: If anyone learns by heart the first ten verses of the Surah al-Kahf, he will be protected from the Dajjal. Sahih Muslim 80

Names of Allah

Al-Muhaymin
The Preserver of Safety

Meal Plan

Suhoor _____

Iftar: _____

Notes

Ramadan Day 8

Todays Goal: **Was it achieved?**

_____   _____

Quran'ic Verse of the Day

وَٱلَّذِينَ يَسْعَوْنَ فِىٓ ءَايَٰتِنَا مُعَٰجِزِينَ أُو۟لَٰٓئِكَ فِى ٱلْعَذَابِ مُحْضَرُونَ

Wallazeena yas'awna feee Aayaatinaa mu'aajizeena ulaaa'ika fil'azaabi muhdaroon

38. And the ones who strive against Our verses to cause [them] failure – those will be brought into the punishment [to remain].

Qur'an Tracker

Juz:
Surah:
Pages ___ **to** ___

Learnt Something New?

_____
_____
_____

Daily Checklist

◯ Fast Completed

◯ Prayed in Mosque: How Many Times

◯ Charitable Donation

◯ Spoke Kind Words all Day

◯ Ate a Healthy Meal

◯ Performed Taraweeh

Cross off prayers upon completion

Fajr
2 Sunnah
2 Fard

Zuhr
4 Sunnah
4 Fard
2 Sunnah

Asr
4 Fard

Maghrib
3 Sunnah
2 Fard

'Isha
4 Sunnah
2 Sunnah

Taraweeh
Rakats:

Tahajjud
Rakats:

Hadith of the Day

Abu Ayub (may Allah be pleased with him) reported that the Prophet (Peace Be Upon Him) said, "Whosoever fasts in Ramadan and then follows it with fasting six days of Shawwal, it is as if he fasts forever." (Muslim)

Names of Allah

Al-Aziz
The Mighty One

Meal Plan

Suhoor _____

Iftar: _____

Notes

Ramadan Day 9

Todays Goal: **Was it achieved?**

_____   _____

Quran'ic Verse of the Day

وَيَوْمَ يَحْشُرُهُمْ جَمِيعًا ثُمَّ يَقُولُ لِلْمَلَٰٓئِكَةِ أَهَٰٓؤُلَآءِ إِيَّاكُمْ كَانُوا۟ يَعْبُدُونَ

Wa yawma yahshuruhum jamee'an summa yaqoolu lilmalaaa'ikati a-haaa'ulaaa'i iyyaakum kaanoo ya'budoon

40. And [mention] the Day when He will gather them all and then say to the angels, "Did these [people] used to worship you?"

Qur'an Tracker

Juz:
Surah:
Pages ____ to ____

Daily Checklist

○ Fast Completed

○ Prayed in Mosque: How Many Times

○ Charitable Donation

○ Spoke Kind Words all Day

○ Ate a Healthy Meal

○ Performed Taraweeh

Learnt Something New?

_____

_____

_____

Cross off prayers upon completion

Fajr
2 Sunnah
2 Fard

Zuhr
4 Sunnah
4 Fard
2 Sunnah

Asr
4 Fard

Maghrib
3 Sunnah
2 Fard

'Isha
4 Sunnah
2 Sunnah

Taraweeh
Rakats:

Tahajjud
Rakats:

Hadith of the Day

Narrated Anas: The Prophet (ﷺ) said, "The real patience is at the first stroke of a calamity." Sahih Al Bukhari 1302, Jami At-Tirmidhi 987 and Sunan an-Nasa'i 1869

Names of Allah

Al-Jabbar
The Omnipotent One

Meal Plan

Suhoor

Iftar:

Notes

Ramadan Day 10

Todays Goal: **Was it achieved?**

_____   _____

Quran'ic Verse of the Day

وَمَآ ءَاتَيْنَٰهُم مِّن كُتُبٍ يَدْرُسُونَهَا ۖ وَمَآ أَرْسَلْنَآ إِلَيْهِمْ قَبْلَكَ مِن نَّذِيرٍ

Wa maaa aatainaahum min Kutubiny yadrusoonahaa wa maaa arsalnaaa ilaihim qablaka min nazeer

44. And We had not given them any scriptures which they could study, and We had not sent to them before you, [O Muhammad], any warner.

Qur'an Tracker

Juz:
Surah:
Pages _____ to _____

Daily Checklist

◯ Fast Completed

◯ Prayed in Mosque: How Many Times

◯ Charitable Donation

◯ Spoke Kind Words all Day

◯ Ate a Healthy Meal

◯ Performed Taraweeh

Learnt Something New?

_____
_____
_____

Cross off prayers upon completion

Fajr
2 Sunnah
2 Fard

Zuhr
4 Sunnah
4 Fard
2 Sunnah

Asr
4 Fard

Maghrib
3 Sunnah
2 Fard

'Isha
4 Sunnah
2 Sunnah

Taraweeh
Rakats:

Tahajjud
Rakats:

Hadith of the Day

Allah's Messenger (ﷺ) said, "If Allah wants to do good to somebody, He afflicts him with trials." Sahih al-Bukhari 5645

Names of Allah

Al-Mutakabbir
The Dominant One

Meal Plan

Suhoor _____

Iftar: _____

Notes

Ramadan Day 11

Todays Goal: **Was it achieved?**

_____   _____

Quran'ic Verse of the Day

قُلْ إِنَّ رَبِّى يَقْذِفُ بِٱلْحَقِّ عَلَّٰمُ ٱلْغُيُوبِ

Qul inna Rabbee yaqzifu bilhaqq 'Allaamul Ghuyoob
48. Say, "Indeed, my Lord projects the truth. Knower of the unseen."

Qur'an Tracker

Juz:
Surah:
Pages ___ **to** ___

Learnt Something New?

_____
_____
_____

Daily Checklist

◯ Fast Completed

◯ Prayed in Mosque: How Many Times

◯ Charitable Donation

◯ Spoke Kind Words all Day

◯ Ate a Healthy Meal

◯ Performed Taraweeh

Cross off prayers upon completion

Fajr
2 Sunnah
2 Fard

Zuhr
4 Sunnah
4 Fard
2 Sunnah

Asr
4 Fard

Maghrib
3 Sunnah
2 Fard

'Isha
4 Sunnah
2 Sunnah

Taraweeh
Rakats:

Tahajjud
Rakats:

Hadith of the Day

Narrated by Abu Huraira: At the time of the Fajr prayer the Prophet asked Bilal, "Tell me of the best deed you did after embracing Islam, for I heard your footsteps in front of me in Paradise." Bilal replied, "I did not do anything worth mentioning except that whenever I performed ablution during the day or night, I prayed after that ablution as much as was written for me." Hadith 250

Names of Allah

Al-Khaaliq
The Creator

Meal Plan

Suhoor _____

Iftar: _____

Notes

Ramadan Day 12

Todays Goal: **Was it achieved?**

_____   _____

Quran'ic Verse of the Day

قُلْ جَاءَ ٱلْحَقُّ وَمَا يُبْدِئُ ٱلْبَاطِلُ وَمَا يُعِيدُ

Qul jaaa'al haqqu wa maa yubdi'ul baatilu wa maa yu'eed

49. Say, "The truth has come, and falsehood can neither begin [anything] nor repeat [it]."

Qur'an Tracker

Juz:
Surah:
Pages ____ to ____

Daily Checklist

○ Fast Completed

○ Prayed in Mosque: How Many Times

○ Charitable Donation

○ Spoke Kind Words all Day

○ Ate a Healthy Meal

○ Performed Taraweeh

Learnt Something New?

_____
_____
_____

Cross off prayers upon completion

Fajr
2 Sunnah
2 Fard

Zuhr
4 Sunnah
4 Fard
2 Sunnah

Asr
4 Fard

Maghrib
3 Sunnah
2 Fard

'Isha
4 Sunnah
2 Sunnah

Taraweeh
Rakats:

Tahajjud
Rakats:

Hadith of the Day

Allah the Exalted says: I have nothing to give to My believing servant other than Paradise if I cause his dear friend to die and he remains patient. Sahih Bukhari 6060

Names of Allah

Al-Baari
The Evolver

Meal Plan

Suhoor _____

Iftar: _____

Notes

Ramadan Day 13

Todays Goal: **Was it achieved?**

_____   _____

Quran'ic Verse of the Day

وَقَدْ كَفَرُواْ بِهِۦ مِن قَبْلُ ۖ وَيَقْذِفُونَ بِٱلْغَيْبِ مِن مَّكَانٍۭ بَعِيدٍ

Wa qad kafaroo bihee min qablu wa yaqzifoona bilghaibi mim makaanim ba'eed

53. And they had already disbelieved in it before and would assault the unseen from a place far away.

Qur'an Tracker

Juz:
Surah:
Pages ____ **to** ____

Daily Checklist

○ **Fast Completed**

○ **Prayed in Mosque: How Many Times**

○ **Charitable Donation**

○ **Spoke Kind Words all Day**

○ **Ate a Healthy Meal**

○ **Performed Taraweeh**

Learnt Something New?

_____

_____

_____

Cross off prayers upon completion

Fajr
2 Sunnah
2 Fard

Zuhr
4 Sunnah
4 Fard
2 Sunnah

Asr
4 Fard

Maghrib
3 Sunnah
2 Fard

'Isha
4 Sunnah
2 Sunnah

Taraweeh
Rakats:

Tahajjud
Rakats:

Hadith of the Day

Al-Aswad narrated: "I asked Aisha what did the Prophet used to do at home. She replied. "He used to keep himself busy serving his family and when it was time for the prayer, he would get up for prayer.""

Names of Allah

Al-Musawwir
The Flawless Shaper

Meal Plan

Suhoor _____

Iftar: _____

Notes

Ramadan Day 14

Todays Goal: **Was it achieved?**

_____   _____

Quran'ic Verse of the Day

وَإِن يُكَذِّبُوكَ فَقَدْ كُذِّبَتْ رُسُلٌ مِّن قَبْلِكَ ۚ وَإِلَى ٱللَّهِ تُرْجَعُ ٱلْأُمُورُ

Wa iny yukazzibooka faqad kuzzibat Rusulum min qablik; wa ilal laahi turja'ul umoor

4. And if they deny you, [O Muhammad] – already were messengers denied before you. And to Allah are returned [all] matters.

Qur'an Tracker

Juz:
Surah:
Pages ____ **to** ____

Learnt Something New?

_____
_____
_____

Daily Checklist

◯ Fast Completed

◯ Prayed in Mosque: How Many Times

◯ Charitable Donation

◯ Spoke Kind Words all Day

◯ Ate a Healthy Meal

◯ Performed Taraweeh

Cross off prayers upon completion

Fajr
2 Sunnah
2 Fard

Zuhr
4 Sunnah
4 Fard
2 Sunnah

Asr
4 Fard

Maghrib
3 Sunnah
2 Fard

'Isha
4 Sunnah
2 Sunnah

Taraweeh
Rakats:

Tahajjud
Rakats:

Hadith of the Day
It was narrated that from Musawir Al Himyari from his mother that she heard Umm Salamah say: "I heard the Messenger of Allah (Peace Be Upon Him) say: 'Any woman who dies when her husband is pleased with her, will enter Paradise.'"

Names of Allah

Al-Ghaffaar
The Great Forgiver

Meal Plan
Suhoor: _____

Iftar: _____

Notes

Ramadan Day 15

Todays Goal: **Was it achieved?**

_____   _____

Quran'ic Verse of the Day

إِنَّ ٱلشَّيْطَٰنَ لَكُمْ عَدُوٌّ فَٱتَّخِذُوهُ عَدُوًّا ۚ إِنَّمَا يَدْعُوا۟ حِزْبَهُۥ لِيَكُونُوا۟ مِنْ أَصْحَٰبِ ٱلسَّعِيرِ

Innash shaitaana lakum 'aduwwun fattakhizoohu 'aduwwaa; innamaa yad'oo hizbahoo liyakoonoo min ashaabis sa'eer

6. Indeed, Satan is an enemy to you; so take him as an enemy. He only invites his party to be among the companions of the Blaze.

Qur'an Tracker

Juz:
Surah:
Pages ____ to ____

Daily Checklist

○ Fast Completed

○ Prayed in Mosque: How Many Times

○ Charitable Donation

○ Spoke Kind Words all Day

○ Ate a Healthy Meal

○ Performed Taraweeh

Learnt Something New?

_____
_____
_____
_____

Cross off prayers upon completion

Fajr
2 Sunnah
2 Fard

Zuhr
4 Sunnah
4 Fard
2 Sunnah

Asr
4 Fard

Maghrib
3 Sunnah
2 Fard

'Isha
4 Sunnah
2 Sunnah

Taraweeh
Rakats:

Tahajjud
Rakats:

Hadith of the Day
Ahmad from Naafi' ibn 'Abd al-Haarith (may Allah be pleased with him) who said: The Messenger of Allaah (Peace Be Upon Him) said: "Part of a man's happiness includes a good neighbour, a comfortable mount, and a spacious abode." Saheeh al-Jaami', no. 3029.

Names of Allah

Al-Qahhaar
The All-Prevailing One

Meal Plan
Suhoor

Iftar:

Notes

Ramadan Day 16

Todays Goal: **Was it achieved?**

_____   _____

Quran'ic Verse of the Day

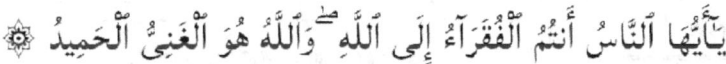

Yaaa ayyunhan naasu antumul fuqaraaa'u ilallaahi wallaahu Huwal Ghaniyyul Hameed

15. O mankind, you are those in need of Allah, while Allah is the Free of need, the Praiseworthy.

Qur'an Tracker

Juz:
Surah:
Pages ____ to ____

Daily Checklist

◯ Fast Completed

◯ Prayed in Mosque: How Many Times

◯ Charitable Donation

◯ Spoke Kind Words all Day

◯ Ate a Healthy Meal

◯ Performed Taraweeh

Learnt Something New?

_____

_____

_____

Cross off prayers upon completion

Fajr
2 Sunnah
2 Fard

Zuhr
4 Sunnah
4 Fard
2 Sunnah

Asr
4 Fard

Maghrib
3 Sunnah
2 Fard

'Isha
4 Sunnah
2 Sunnah

Taraweeh
Rakats:

Tahajjud
Rakats:

Hadith of the Day

Bukhari and Muslim narrate the following: "None of you will believe until you love for your brother what you love for yourself."

Names of Allah

Al-Wahhab
The Supreme Bestower

Meal Plan

Suhoor

Iftar:

Notes

Ramadan Day 17

Todays Goal: **Was it achieved?**

_____   _____

Quran'ic Verse of the Day

إِن يَشَأْ يُذْهِبْكُمْ وَيَأْتِ بِخَلْقٍ جَدِيدٍ

Iny yashaa yuzhibkum wa yaati bikhalqin jadeed
16. If He wills, He can do away with you and bring forth a new creation.

Qur'an Tracker

Juz:
Surah:
Pages ___ **to** ___

Learnt Something New?

_____
_____
_____

Daily Checklist

◯ Fast Completed

◯ Prayed in Mosque: How Many Times

◯ Charitable Donation

◯ Spoke Kind Words all Day

◯ Ate a Healthy Meal

◯ Performed Taraweeh

Cross off prayers upon completion

Fajr
2 Sunnah
2 Fard

Zuhr
4 Sunnah
4 Fard
2 Sunnah

Asr
4 Fard

Maghrib
3 Sunnah
2 Fard

'Isha
4 Sunnah
2 Sunnah

Taraweeh
Rakats:

Tahajjud
Rakats:

Hadith of the Day

"He who believes in Allah and the Last Day must either speak good or remain silent." - Muslim

Names of Allah

Ar-Razzaq
The Total Provider

Meal Plan

Suhoor _____

Iftar: _____
_____

Notes
_____
_____
_____
_____

Ramadan Day 18

Todays Goal: **Was it achieved?**

_____   _____

Quran'ic Verse of the Day

وَمَا ذَٰلِكَ عَلَى ٱللَّهِ بِعَزِيزٍ

Wa maa zaalika 'alal laahi bi'azeez
17. And that is for Allah not difficult.

Qur'an Tracker

Juz:
Surah:
Pages _____ **to** _____

Learnt Something New?

_____
_____
_____

Daily Checklist

○ Fast Completed

○ Prayed in Mosque: How Many Times

○ Charitable Donation

○ Spoke Kind Words all Day

○ Ate a Healthy Meal

○ Performed Taraweeh

Cross off prayers upon completion

Fajr
2 Sunnah
2 Fard

Zuhr
4 Sunnah
4 Fard
2 Sunnah

Asr
4 Fard

Maghrib
3 Sunnah
2 Fard

'Isha
4 Sunnah
2 Sunnah

Taraweeh
Rakats:

Tahajjud
Rakats:

Hadith of the Day

"If anyone fulfils his brother's needs, Allah will fulfil his needs; if one relieves a Muslim of his troubles, Allah will relieve his troubles on the Day of Resurrection." [Prophet Muhammad (Peace Be Upon Him), Sahih Bukhari].

Names of Allah

Al-Fattah
The Supreme Solver

Meal Plan

Suhoor _____

Iftar: _____

Notes

Ramadan Day 19

Todays Goal: **Was it achieved?**

_____   _____

Quran'ic Verse of the Day

ثُمَّ أَخَذْتُ ٱلَّذِينَ كَفَرُوا۟ فَكَيْفَ كَانَ نَكِيرِ

Summa akhaztul lazeena kafaroo fakaifa kaana nakeer (section 3)
26. Then I seized the ones who disbelieved, and how [terrible] was My reproach.

Qur'an Tracker

Juz:
Surah:
Pages ____ to ____

Learnt Something New?

_____
_____
_____

Daily Checklist

○ Fast Completed

○ Prayed in Mosque: How Many Times

○ Charitable Donation

○ Spoke Kind Words all Day

○ Ate a Healthy Meal

○ Performed Taraweeh

Cross off prayers upon completion

Fajr
2 Sunnah
2 Fard

Zuhr
4 Sunnah
4 Fard
2 Sunnah

Asr
4 Fard

Maghrib
3 Sunnah
2 Fard

'Isha
4 Sunnah
2 Sunnah

Taraweeh
Rakats:

Tahajjud
Rakats:

Hadith of the Day

Abu Huraira reported: The Messenger of Allah (Peace Be Upon Him), said: "Verily, Allah will say on the Day of Resurrection: Where are those who love each other for the sake of my glory? Today, I will shelter them in my shade on a day when there is no shade but mine." [Prophet Muhammad pbuh, Ṣaḥīḥ Muslim 2566].

Names of Allah

Al-Qaabid
The Restricting One

Meal Plan

Suhoor

Iftar:

Notes

Ramadan Day 20

Todays Goal: **Was it achieved?**

_____   _____

Quran'ic Verse of the Day

فَمَا كَانَ دَعْوَىٰهُمْ إِذْ جَاءَهُم بَأْسُنَا إِلَّا أَن قَالُوا إِنَّا كُنَّا ظَالِمِينَ

Famaa kaana da'waahum iz jaaa'ahum baasunaa illaaa an qaalooo innaa kunnaa zaalimeen

5. And their declaration when Our punishment came to them was only that they said, "Indeed, we were wrongdoers!"

Qur'an Tracker

Juz:
Surah:
Pages ____ **to** ____

Daily Checklist

○ Fast Completed

○ Prayed in Mosque: How Many Times

○ Charitable Donation

○ Spoke Kind Words all Day

○ Ate a Healthy Meal

○ Performed Taraweeh

Learnt Something New?

_____
_____
_____

Cross off prayers upon completion

Fajr
2 Sunnah
2 Fard

Zuhr
4 Sunnah
4 Fard
2 Sunnah

Asr
4 Fard

Maghrib
3 Sunnah
2 Fard

'Isha
4 Sunnah
2 Sunnah

Taraweeh
Rakats:

Tahajjud
Rakats:

Hadith of the Day

It is reported that Abū Hurayrah - Allāh be pleased with him - used to say: Whoever does not think that his speech is part of his deeds and that his character is part of his religion will be destroyed without even realizing. Ibn Abī Al-Dunyā Dham Al-Kadhib wa Ahlī article 94.

Names of Allah

Al-Baasit
The Extender

Meal Plan

Suhoor _____

Iftar: _____

Notes

Ramadan Day 21

Todays Goal: **Was it achieved?**

_____   _____

Quran'ic Verse of the Day

فَلَنَسْـَٔلَنَّ ٱلَّذِينَ أُرْسِلَ إِلَيْهِمْ وَلَنَسْـَٔلَنَّ ٱلْمُرْسَلِينَ

Falanas 'alannal lazeena ursila ilaihim wa lanas 'alannal mursaleen

6. Then We will surely question those to whom [a message] was sent, and We will surely question the messengers.

Qur'an Tracker

Juz:
Surah:
Pages ____ to ____

Daily Checklist

○ Fast Completed

○ Prayed in Mosque: How Many Times

○ Charitable Donation

○ Spoke Kind Words all Day

○ Ate a Healthy Meal

○ Performed Taraweeh

Learnt Something New?

_____
_____
_____

Cross off prayers upon completion

Fajr
2 Sunnah
2 Fard

Zuhr
4 Sunnah
4 Fard
2 Sunnah

Asr
4 Fard

Maghrib
3 Sunnah
2 Fard

'Isha
4 Sunnah
2 Sunnah

Taraweeh
Rakats:

Tahajjud
Rakats:

Hadith of the Day

Allah's Apostle said, "If a dog drinks from the utensil of anyone of you it is essential to wash it seven times." Hadith No: 173 Narrated/Authority of Abu Huraira

Names of Allah

Al-Khaafid
The Reducer

Meal Plan

Suhoor

Iftar:

Notes

Ramadan Day 22

Todays Goal: **Was it achieved?**

_____   _____

Quran'ic Verse of the Day

فَلَنَقُصَّنَّ عَلَيْهِم بِعِلْمٍ ۖ وَمَا كُنَّا غَآئِبِينَ

Falanaqussanna 'alaihim bi'ilminw wa maa kunnaa ghaaa'ibeen

7. Then We will surely relate [their deeds] to them with knowledge, and We were not [at all] absent.

Qur'an Tracker

Juz:
Surah:
Pages ____ to ____

Learnt Something New?

_____
_____
_____

Daily Checklist

◯ Fast Completed

◯ Prayed in Mosque: How Many Times

◯ Charitable Donation

◯ Spoke Kind Words all Day

◯ Ate a Healthy Meal

◯ Performed Taraweeh

Cross off prayers upon completion

Fajr
2 Sunnah
2 Fard

Zuhr
4 Sunnah
4 Fard
2 Sunnah

Asr
4 Fard

Maghrib
3 Sunnah
2 Fard

'Isha
4 Sunnah
2 Sunnah

Taraweeh
Rakats:

Tahajjud
Rakats:

Hadith of the Day

Narrated by Abu Huraira: The Prophet (Peace Be Upon Him) said, "A wound which a Muslim receives in Allah's cause will appear on the Day of Resurrection as it was at the time of infliction; blood will be flowing from the wound and its color will be that of the blood but will smell like musk."

Hadith No: 238

Names of Allah

Ar-Rafi
The Elevating One

Meal Plan

Suhoor _____

Iftar: _____

Notes

Ramadan Day 23

Todays Goal: **Was it achieved?**

_____ _____

Quran'ic Verse of the Day

قَالَ فَبِمَآ أَغْوَيْتَنِى لَأَقْعُدَنَّ لَهُمْ صِرَٰطَكَ ٱلْمُسْتَقِيمَ

Qaala fabimaaa aghway tanee la aqudanna lahum Siraatakal Mustaqeem

16. [Satan] said, "Because You have put me in error, I will surely sit in wait for them on Your straight path.

Qur'an Tracker

Juz:
Surah:
Pages ___ to ___

Learnt Something New?

_____
_____
_____

Daily Checklist

◯ Fast Completed

◯ Prayed in Mosque: How Many Times

◯ Charitable Donation

◯ Spoke Kind Words all Day

◯ Ate a Healthy Meal

◯ Performed Taraweeh

Cross off prayers upon completion

Fajr
2 Sunnah
2 Fard

Zuhr
4 Sunnah
4 Fard
2 Sunnah

Asr
4 Fard

Maghrib
3 Sunnah
2 Fard

'Isha
4 Sunnah
2 Sunnah

Taraweeh
Rakats:

Tahajjud
Rakats:

Hadith of the Day

The Prophet (Peace Be Upon Him) said, "If anyone of you stands for prayer, he should not spit in front of him because in prayer he is speaking in private to Allah and he should not spit on his right as there is an angel, but he can spit either on his left or under his left foot and bury it (i.e. expectoration)."
Hadith No: 408 Narrated by Abu Huraira,

Names of Allah

Al-Mu'izz
The Honourer-Bestower

Meal Plan

Suhoor _____

Iftar: _____
_____

Notes

Ramadan Day 24

Todays Goal: **Was it achieved?**

_____   _____

Quran'ic Verse of the Day

وَقَاسَمَهُمَآ إِنِّى لَكُمَا لَمِنَ ٱلنَّـٰصِحِينَ

Wa qaasamahumaaa innee lakumaa laminan naasiheen

21. And he swore [by Allah] to them, "Indeed, I am to you from among the sincere advisors

Qur'an Tracker

Juz:
Surah:
Pages ____ **to** ____

Learnt Something New?

_____
_____
_____

Daily Checklist

◯ Fast Completed

◯ Prayed in Mosque: How Many Times

◯ Charitable Donation

◯ Spoke Kind Words all Day

◯ Ate a Healthy Meal

◯ Performed Taraweeh

Cross off prayers upon completion

Fajr
2 Sunnah
2 Fard

Zuhr
4 Sunnah
4 Fard
2 Sunnah

Asr
4 Fard

Maghrib
3 Sunnah
2 Fard

'Isha
4 Sunnah
2 Sunnah

Taraweeh
Rakats:

Tahajjud
Rakats:

Hadith of the Day
Narrated by Abu Huraira
I heard Allah's Apostle saying, "If there was a river at the door of anyone of you and he took a bath in it five times a day would you notice any dirt on him?" They said, "Not a trace of dirt would be left." The Prophet added, "That is the example of the five prayers with which Allah blots out (annuls) evil deeds." Hadith No: 506

Names of Allah

Al-Muzil
The Abaser

Meal Plan

Suhoor _____

Iftar: _____

Notes

Ramadan Day 25

Todays Goal: **Was it achieved?**

_____   _____

Quran'ic Verse of the Day

قَالَ فِيهَا تَحْيَوْنَ وَفِيهَا تَمُوتُونَ وَمِنْهَا تُخْرَجُونَ

Qaala feehaa tahyawna wa feehaa tamootoona wa minhaa tukhrajoon (section 2)

25. He said, "Therein you will live, and therein you will die, and from it you will be brought forth

Qur'an Tracker

Juz:
Surah:
Pages ____ **to** ____

Learnt Something New?

_____

_____

_____

Daily Checklist

◯ **Fast Completed**

◯ **Prayed in Mosque: How Many Times**

◯ **Charitable Donation**

◯ **Spoke Kind Words all Day**

◯ **Ate a Healthy Meal**

◯ **Performed Taraweeh**

Cross off prayers upon completion

Fajr
2 Sunnah
2 Fard

Zuhr
4 Sunnah
4 Fard
2 Sunnah

Asr
4 Fard

Maghrib
3 Sunnah
2 Fard

'Isha
4 Sunnah
2 Sunnah

Taraweeh
Rakats:

Tahajjud
Rakats:

Hadith of the Day

Narrated by Abu Huraira Allah's Apostle said, "Angels come to you in succession by night and day and all of them get together at the time of the Fajr and 'Asr prayers. Those who have passed the night with you (or stayed with you) ascend (to the Heaven) and Allah asks them, though He knows everything about you, well, "In what state did you leave my slaves?" The angels reply: "When we left them they were praying and when we reached them, they were praying."

Names of Allah

As-Sami'
The All-Hearer

Meal Plan

Suhoor _____

Iftar: _____

Notes

Ramadan Day 26

Todays Goal: **Was it achieved?**

_____   _____

Quran'ic Verse of the Day

وَلَقَدْ صَدَّقَ عَلَيْهِمْ إِبْلِيسُ ظَنَّهُ فَاتَّبَعُوهُ إِلَّا فَرِيقًا مِّنَ ٱلْمُؤْمِنِينَ

Wa laqad saddaq 'alaihim Ibleesu zannnabhoo fattaba'oohu illaa fareeqam minal mu'mineen

20. And Iblees had already confirmed through them his assumption, so they followed him, except for a party of believers.

Qur'an Tracker

Juz:
Surah:
Pages ___ **to** ___

Learnt Something New?

_____
_____
_____

Daily Checklist

◯ Fast Completed

◯ Prayed in Mosque: How Many Times

◯ Charitable Donation

◯ Spoke Kind Words all Day

◯ Ate a Healthy Meal

◯ Performed Taraweeh

Cross off prayers upon completion

Fajr
2 Sunnah
2 Fard

Zuhr
4 Sunnah
4 Fard
2 Sunnah

Asr
4 Fard

Maghrib
3 Sunnah
2 Fard

'Isha
4 Sunnah
2 Sunnah

Taraweeh
Rakats:

Tahajjud
Rakats:

Hadith of the Day
Narrated by Abu Huraira Allah's Apostle said, "If anyone of you can get one Rak'a of the 'Asr prayer before sunset, he should complete his prayer. If any of you can get one Rak'a of the Fajr prayer before sunrise, he should complete his prayer."

Names of Allah

Al-Hakam
The Impartial Judge

Meal Plan
Suhoor: _____

Iftar: _____

Notes

Ramadan Day 27

Todays Goal: **Was it achieved?**

_____   _____

Quran'ic Verse of the Day

وَقَالَتْ أُولَىٰهُمْ لِأُخْرَىٰهُمْ فَمَا كَانَ لَكُمْ عَلَيْنَا مِن فَضْلٍ فَذُوقُوا۟ ٱلْعَذَابَ بِمَا كُنتُمْ تَكْسِبُونَ

Wa qaalat oolaahum li ukhraahum famaa kaana lakum 'alainaa min fadlin fazooqul azaaba bimaa kuntum taksiboon (section 4)

39. And the first of them will say to the last of them, "Then you had not any favor over us, so taste the punishment for what you used to earn

Qur'an Tracker

Juz:
Surah:
Pages ____ to ____

Learnt Something New?

_____

_____

_____

Daily Checklist

◯ Fast Completed

◯ Prayed in Mosque: How Many Times

◯ Charitable Donation

◯ Spoke Kind Words all Day

◯ Ate a Healthy Meal

◯ Performed Taraweeh

Cross off prayers upon completion

Fajr
2 Sunnah
2 Fard

Zuhr
4 Sunnah
4 Fard
2 Sunnah

Asr
4 Fard

Maghrib
3 Sunnah
2 Fard

'Isha
4 Sunnah
2 Sunnah

Taraweeh
Rakats:

Tahajjud
Rakats:

Hadith of the Day

Narrated by Abu Huraira: The Prophet (Peace Be Upon Him) said, "Isn't he who raises his head before the Imam afraid that Allah may transform his head into that of a donkey or his figure (face) into that of a donkey?"
Hadith No: 660

Names of Allah

Al-Adl
The Embodiment of Justice

Meal Plan

Suhoor _____

Iftar: _____

Notes

Ramadan Day 28

Todays Goal: **Was it achieved?**

_____   _____

Quran'ic Verse of the Day

لَهُم مِّن جَهَنَّمَ مِهَادٌ وَمِن فَوْقِهِمْ غَوَاشٍ ۚ وَكَذَٰلِكَ نَجْزِي ٱلظَّٰلِمِينَ

Lahum min jahannama mihaadunw wa min fawqihim ghawaash;
wa kazaalika najziz zaalimeen

41. They will have from Hell a bed and over them coverings [of fire]. And thus do We recompense the wrongdoers.

Qur'an Tracker

Juz:
Surah:
Pages ___ to ___

Learnt Something New?

_____

_____

_____

Daily Checklist

◯ Fast Completed

◯ Prayed in Mosque: How Many Times

◯ Charitable Donation

◯ Spoke Kind Words all Day

◯ Ate a Healthy Meal

◯ Performed Taraweeh

Cross off prayers upon completion

Fajr
2 Sunnah
2 Fard

Zuhr
4 Sunnah
4 Fard
2 Sunnah

Asr
4 Fard

Maghrib
3 Sunnah
2 Fard

'Isha
4 Sunnah
2 Sunnah

Taraweeh
Rakats:

Tahajjud
Rakats:

Hadith of the Day

Narrated by Abu Huraira: I heard Allah's Apostles (Peace Be Upon Him) saying, "If the prayer is started do not run for it but just walk for it calmly and pray whatever you get, and complete whatever is missed." Hadith No: 31

Names of Allah

Al-Lateef
The Knower of Subtleties

Meal Plan

Suhoor

Iftar:

Notes

Ramadan Day 29

Todays Goal: **Was it achieved?**

_____   _____

Quran'ic Verse of the Day

ٱلَّذِينَ يَصُدُّونَ عَن سَبِيلِ ٱللَّهِ وَيَبْغُونَهَا عِوَجًا وَهُم بِٱلْءَاخِرَةِ كَٰفِرُونَ

Allazeena yasuddoona 'an sabeelil laahi wa yabghoo nahaa 'iwajanw wa hum bil Aakhirati kaafiroon

Ayat 45. Who averted [people] from the way of Allah and sought to make it [seem] deviant while they were, concerning the Hereafter, disbelievers.

Qur'an Tracker

Juz:
Surah:
Pages ____ to ____

Learnt Something New?

_____
_____
_____

Daily Checklist

◯ Fast Completed

◯ Prayed in Mosque: How Many Times

◯ Charitable Donation

◯ Spoke Kind Words all Day

◯ Ate a Healthy Meal

◯ Performed Taraweeh

Cross off prayers upon completion

Fajr
2 Sunnah
2 Fard

Zuhr
4 Sunnah
4 Fard
2 Sunnah

Asr
4 Fard

Maghrib
3 Sunnah
2 Fard

'Isha
4 Sunnah
2 Sunnah

Taraweeh
Rakats:

Tahajjud
Rakats:

Hadith of the Day

Narrated by Abu Huraira. Allah's Apostle (Peace Be Upon Him) said, "When the Imam is delivering the Khutba, and you ask your companion to keep quiet and listen, then no doubt you have done an evil act." Hadith No: 56

Names of Allah

Al-Khabeer
The All-Aware One

Meal Plan

Suhoor _____

Iftar: _____

Notes

Ramadan Day 30

Todays Goal: **Was it achieved?**

_____   _____

Quran'ic Verse of the Day

ٱدْعُواْ رَبَّكُمْ تَضَرُّعًا وَخُفْيَةً ۚ إِنَّهُ لَا يُحِبُّ ٱلْمُعْتَدِينَ

Udoo Rabbakum tadarruanw wa khufyah; innahoo laa yuhibbul mutadeen

55. Call upon your Lord in humility and privately; indeed, He does not like transgressors.

Qur'an Tracker

Juz:
Surah:
Pages ____ to ____

Daily Checklist

○ Fast Completed

○ Prayed in Mosque: How Many Times

○ Charitable Donation

○ Spoke Kind Words all Day

○ Ate a Healthy Meal

○ Performed Taraweeh

Learnt Something New?

_____
_____
_____

Cross off prayers upon completion

Fajr
2 Sunnah
2 Fard

Zuhr
4 Sunnah
4 Fard
2 Sunnah

Asr
4 Fard

Maghrib
3 Sunnah
2 Fard

'Isha
4 Sunnah
2 Sunnah

Taraweeh
Rakats:

Tahajjud
Rakats:

Hadith of the Day

Narrated by Abu Huraira. Allah's Apostle (Peace Be Upon Him) talked about Friday and said, "There is an hour (opportune time) on Friday and if a Muslim gets it while praying and asks something from Allah, then Allah will definitely meet his demand." And he (the Prophet) pointed out the shortness of that time with his hands. Hadith No: 57

Names of Allah

Al-Baseer
The All-Seeing

Meal Plan

Suhoor _____

Iftar: _____

Notes

"Whoever says 'SubhanAllah wa bihamdihi' one hundred times a day will be forgiven all his sins, even if they were as much as the foam of the sea." *Bukhari.*

Monthly Recap

Use the following pages to note down everything you have learnt over this month.

The aim of this is to monitor your progress with the other Islamic months. This will help you to observe your improvements and progress enabling you to have an overview of your growth within your Deen.

Aim to learn and apply new positive habits every month.

By the end of the month, review all of your progress. For example, if you have learnt a new surah, then recite it repeatedly throughout the day on the last day of the month in order to reinforce its memorisation.

Notes

Notes

This is a truly unique and educational journal - unlike anything on the market right now. Our goal when creating this journal series was to serve the Ummah in an invaluable way. We were sincerely concerned with the way in which fellow Muslims would eat during Ramadan. Having not only focused on the fasting and praying element of Ramadan, we have set out to make it as informative as possible, with a detailed look at how to maximise the health and spiritual benefits of this sacred month. Improving your habits was another focus of ours.

Hadiths and prophetic methodologies have been explored alongside scientific findings and results from clients - all with the intention of bringing us back to the dietary protocol that was intended for us. Putting all of this beneficial knowledge into practice is a core aim of these journals, which have been designed in a way to support your development, growth and progress. By adopting this new diet and routine, you will insha'Allah experience first hand the improvements that our clients have achieved.

Our daily trackers allow you to consistently track your Islamic progress day after day. It will help you oversee stagnant days and also active days thus enabling you to monitor yourself effectively. This tracker is aimed at encouraging you to achieve and learn something new everyday, even if it is small - we want you to be moving forward all the time. We must strive in our life to follow the ways of the Prophet Muhammad (PBUH) and those that surrounded him so that we too can be granted Jannatul-Firdaus, Insha'Allah.

There are 12 books in our series; one for each Islamic lunar month, each including a daily tracker. Each book will focus on different health topics that are commonly addressed in our community and how to implement this knowledge into your day to day lives. We also include other Sunnah practices that our beloved Prophet (PBUH) lived by, whilst using the tracker to record new habits.

Good luck on your journey!

Asalam-U-Alaykum

www.ingramcontent.com/pod-product-compliance
Lightning Source LLC
Chambersburg PA
CBHW070437010526
44118CB00014B/2077